**W9-BWX-138**

BOUNDARIES
PARTICIPANT'S GUIDE — REVISED

Resources by Henry Cloud and John Townsend

Books

Boundaries (and workbook)
Boundaries in Dating (and workbook)
Boundaries in Marriage (and workbook)
Boundaries with Kids (and workbook)
Boundaries with Teens (Townsend)
Changes That Heal (and workbook) (Cloud)
Hiding from Love (Townsend)
How People Grow (and workbook)
How to Have That Difficult Conversation You've Been Avoiding
Making Small Groups Work
The Mom Factor (and workbook)
Raising Great Kids
Raising Great Kids Workbook for Parents of Preschoolers
Raising Great Kids Workbook for Parents of School-Age Children
Raising Great Kids Workbook for Parents of Teenagers
Safe People (and workbook)
12 "Christian" Beliefs That Can Drive You Crazy

Video Curriculum

Boundaries
Boundaries in Dating
Boundaries in Marriage
Boundaries with Kids
Raising Great Kids for Parents of Preschoolers
ReGroup (with Bill Donahue)

Audio

Boundaries
Boundaries in Dating
Boundaries in Marriage
Boundaries with Kids
Boundaries with Teens (Townsend)
Changes That Heal (Cloud)
How People Grow
How to Have That Difficult Conversation You've Been Avoiding
Making Small Groups Work
The Mom Factor
Raising Great Kids

BOUNDARIES

PARTICIPANT'S GUIDE – REVISED

WHEN TO SAY YES
HOW TO SAY NO
TO TAKE CONTROL
OF YOUR LIFE

DR. HENRY CLOUD & DR. JOHN TOWNSEND

WITH LISA GUEST

ZONDERVAN®

ZONDERVAN.com/
AUTHORTRACKER
follow your favorite authors

We want to hear from you. Please send your comments about this book to us in care of zreview@zondervan.com. Thank you.

ZONDERVAN®

Boundaries Participant's Guide — Revised
Copyright © 2007 by Henry Cloud and John Townsend

Requests for information should be addressed to:

Zondervan, *Grand Rapids, Michigan 49530*

ISBN-10: 0-310-27808-2
ISBN-13: 978-0-310-27808-5

All Scripture quotations, unless otherwise indicated, are taken from the *Holy Bible, New International Version*®. NIV®. Copyright © 1973, 1978, 1984 by International Bible Society. Used by permission of Zondervan. All rights reserved.

Scripture marked NASB is taken from the *New American Standard Bible*. Copyright © 1960, 1962, 1963, 1968, 1971, 1972, 1973, 1975, 1977, 1995 by The Lockman Foundation. Used by permission.

Internet addresses (websites, blogs, etc.) and telephone numbers printed in this book are offered as a resource to you. These are not intended in any way to be or imply an endorsement on the part of Zondervan, nor do we vouch for the content of these sites and numbers for the life of this book.

Published in association with Yates & Yates, LLP, Attorneys and Counselors, Suite 1000, Literary Agent, Orange, CA

Interior design by Beth Shagene

Printed in the United States of America

08 09 10 11 12 13 • 24 23 22 21 20 19 18 17 16 15 14 13 12 11 10 9 8 7 6 5 4

Contents

Preface

*M*any people who want to have healthy lives are unsure about when it is appropriate to say no and set limits. They want to have good relationships and grow spiritually, but they often find it difficult to take ownership of their choices, freedom, and responsibilities. In a word, they do not have good boundaries.

When confronted about their lack of boundaries, these people raise important questions:

- Can I set limits and still be a loving person?
- What are legitimate boundaries?
- What if my boundaries upset or hurt someone?
- What can I say to someone who wants my time, love, energy, or money?
- Why do I feel guilty or afraid when I consider setting boundaries?
- Are boundaries selfish?
- Why is it difficult for me to hear no from people?
- Do I sometimes try to control or manipulate people when I don't get what I want?

This small-group curriculum presents a biblical view of boundaries: what they are, what they protect, how they are developed, how they are injured, how to repair them, and how to use them. Our goal is to help you use healthy boundaries appropriately to achieve the relationships and purposes that God intends for you. We want to help you see how boundaries operate in relationships, in tasks, and in your spiritual life.

God bless you.

HENRY CLOUD, PHD
JOHN TOWNSEND, PHD

What Is a Boundary?

*I*n this session you will:

- Define what boundaries are and why they are important
- Identify some examples of boundaries
- Find out what you are responsible for within your boundaries
- Learn that the concept of boundaries comes from the nature of God himself
- Discover how boundaries result in freedom and how freedom leads to love

Learning Together

DVD Segment #1: "Sherrie Without Boundaries"

For the next nine sessions, we are going to look at boundaries—what they are and how they can help us experience healthy relationships, love, and freedom. Sometimes it's easier to understand what something *is* by seeing what it is *not*—and that's what our opening DVD segment, titled "Sherrie Without Boundaries," will show us.

- Sherrie is trying to do a good job with her marriage, her children, her job, and her relationships. Yet it's obvious that something isn't right. Life isn't working.

- Sherrie isn't able to draw and maintain boundaries around what is hers, boundaries that would help keep out what isn't hers.

- In the physical world, boundaries are easy to see, and they give the message: THIS IS WHERE MY PROPERTY BEGINS. The owner of the property is legally responsible for what happens on his or her own property. Nonowners are not responsible for the property.

- Just as homeowners set physical property lines around their property, we need to set mental, physical, emotional, and spiritual boundaries for our lives to help us distinguish what is our responsibility and what isn't.

- A variety of things, including past hurts, poor models, and misunderstood teachings, result in weak boundaries or in boundaries that don't exist at all.

- Boundaries define what is me and what is not me. A boundary shows where each individual ends and someone else begins, leading each person to a sense of ownership and responsibility. Boundaries also protect us from the bad.

Talking Together

Examples of Boundaries

1. What did you find most striking about Sherrie and the way her life was going?

2. In what ways—if any—are you, like Sherrie, living life without boundaries? Be specific.

3. In what areas of life do you have boundaries but wish they were stronger? Again, be specific.

Boundaries help us differentiate ourselves from someone else; they show where each person begins and ends. Right now we're going to look at some examples of boundaries.

4. Living life with healthy boundaries begins by first simply
   identifying boundaries. Following is a list of some important
   boundaries. Turn to one or two people near you and tell them
   which of these items, if any, you were surprised to see on the
   list. Why do you think you never thought about those as being
   boundaries?

   - *Skin* (yes, literally, the skin on your body)

   - *Words* (especially the word *no*)

   - *Truth* (about God and about who you are)

   - *Time* (Time, as in "time away from," can be healthy.)

   - *Geographical distance* (Remove yourself from a situation.)

   - *Emotional distance* (Guard your heart.)

   - *Other people* (They are not you—and they can help you set
     and keep boundaries!)

   - *Consequences* (Setting and enforcing consequences will show
     people that you're serious about keeping your boundaries.)

Now, as a group, answer these two questions:

5. Think about a time when someone did not honor a boundary you set. What prevents you from keeping your boundaries strong?

6. Now consider boundaries from the opposite perspective. What will you do to be more respectful of the boundaries of people in your life?

Boundary Building ... On Your Own

For You to Do After This Session and Before the Next One

1. Think of a time when you stuck by one of your boundaries and people respected it. What were the circumstances? Why were you able to maintain your boundary?

2. Now think back to the group's responses to the question, "What prevents you from keeping your boundaries strong?" Which answer given in that discussion best explains why you aren't always able to maintain your boundaries? And what will you do to strengthen your boundary-keeping ability? What step in that direction will you take this week?

3. Why might you have a hard time honoring people's boundaries, especially certain people's? What will you do to be more respectful of those people and their boundaries? Be specific.

The Responsibilities That Come with Boundaries

Having identified boundaries, now we need to look more closely at what falls within our boundaries, at what we are responsible for. Following is a list of some of what each one of us is responsible for. Discuss your answers to questions 1–9 below with two or three of the people sitting near you.

- Our feelings
- Our attitudes/beliefs/desires
- Our behaviors
- Our choices
- Our values
- Our thoughts
- Our limits
- Our talents
- Our love/trust

1. Ignoring *feelings* or letting them rule over us is not being responsible for them. What does being responsible for feelings look like?

2. When have you seen a person's *attitude or belief* cause that person to make poor choices and/or experience pain? What would have been a responsible alternative?

3. What *behaviors* do we—do you—tend to blame or at least want to blame on other people or on circumstances? Why is blaming not a responsible course of action?

4. What can make us feel that we don't have a *choice* in a situation when we actually do? Again, why is it not responsible to let yourself believe that you don't have a choice?

5. Why is it unwise to *value* the approval of people rather than the approval of God (John 12:43)? Give a real-life example that illustrates the futility of valuing people's approval.

6. What specific aspects of life would each of us do well to *think* through for ourselves?

7. What kind of evils is it wise for us to *limit* our exposure to?
Identify subtle evils, not just obvious ones. In addition to setting
limits with others—with people whose presence in our life
destroys love—we need to set internal limits. What does such
self-control without repression look like? Give an example
or two.

8. What *talent*, gift, or ability are you being a wise steward of?
Share one example.

9. What can we do to open ourselves to receiving more of God's
love? What can each of us do to be a more effective channel of
God's love?

Boundary Building ... On Your Own

For You to Do After This Session and Before the Next One

1. What do you tend to do with your *feelings* — ignore them or let them be in charge? Why do you think you respond the way you do?

2. What *attitude* and/or *belief* is causing you to make poor choices or experience pain? What will you do to get that attitude or belief in line with God's truth?

3. What *desires* are you currently pursuing that your heavenly Father, wise parent that he is, is probably not interested in giving you? What destructive desires do you need to learn to say no to? Also, what good desires do you need to say no to because the timing isn't right?

4. What unhealthy, unhelpful, insensitive, or sinful *behaviors* do you need to take responsibility for? What will that look like? Be specific.

5. What *choice* in your life have you failed to take responsibility for? Also, whom are you blaming for what circumstances in your life?

6. Identify evidence in your life that shows which you *value* more: people's approval or God's approval. Consider a decision you currently face. Which source of approval is exerting more pull on you?

7. Whom are you expecting to read your mind, or to whom are you afraid to communicate your *thoughts*? What keeps you from doing so?

8. Whom in your life would you be wise to *limit* your exposure to? What is keeping you from doing so?

9. What *talent*, gift, or ability are you afraid to exercise? What step will you take to overcome that fear?

10. What healthy, godly relationships nurture you? To whom are you giving the kind of unconditional *love* God gives you?

Exploring Together

Responsible To, Responsible For

We've looked at examples of boundaries and at the responsibilities that come with boundaries. Now let's explore a few more foundational facts about boundaries and then discuss together the questions that follow.

As we've seen, boundaries help us distinguish our property so that we can take care of it—and we *are* responsible for taking care of it. We need to keep things that will nurture us inside our fences and keep things that will harm us outside. In short, boundaries help us keep the good in and the bad out. But these fences need to have gates so that we can let the good in and let out any bad.

This concept of boundaries comes from the very nature of God. God defines himself as a distinct being separate from his creation and from us. He has boundaries within the Trinity. The Father, the Son, and the Spirit are one, but at the same time they are distinct persons with their own boundaries.

God also limits what he will allow in his yard. He confronts sin and allows consequences for behavior. He guards his house and will not allow evil things to go on there. He invites people in who will love him, and he lets his love flow outward to them at the same time. Created in God's likeness, we have personal responsibilities within limits, within the boundaries that we set and maintain.

Talking Together

The Right Kind of Responsibility

1. What encouragement to set and maintain boundaries do you find in the description of God's nature found in "Exploring Together"?

2. Keeping in mind what you learned in "Exploring Together," read aloud Galatians 6:1 – 5 as a group.

   What does Galatians 6:2 teach about our responsibility *to* one another?

   What does Galatians 6:5 teach about being responsible *for* ourselves?

When has someone in your life followed Christ's example of sacrificial love and denied him- or herself in order to do for you what you could not do for yourself?

What current opportunity do you have to deny yourself in order to do for others what they cannot do for themselves? Let your group pray for you and hold you accountable to taking this step of sacrificial love.

The Greek word for *burden* means "excess burdens" or boulders that we need help carrying. The Greek word for *load* means "the burden of daily toil," something like a knapsack that we are able and expected to carry on our own. Likewise, we are expected to deal with our own feelings, attitudes, behaviors, and God-given responsibilities even though it takes effort.

Boundary Building ... On Your Own

For You to Do After This Session and Before the Next One

1. What specific aspect of God's healthy boundaries (paragraphs 3 and 4 of "Responsible *To*, Responsible *For*" on page 19) is especially significant for you? Why?

2. In what situations today are you acting as if *boulders* in your life are your daily load and refusing to seek and/or to accept offers of help that people have extended to you?

3. In what situations today are you acting as if the *burden of daily toil* is a boulder you shouldn't have to carry?

4. What have these two questions helped you to see about yourself — and what will you do as a result of that insight?

Learning Together

DVD Segment #2: "Wrapping It Up"

We're going to conclude our session by hearing a little bit more from Dr. Cloud and Dr. Townsend.

- Made in the image of God, we were created to take responsibility for certain tasks. Part of taking responsibility, or ownership, is knowing what *is* our job and what *isn't*. It takes wisdom to know what we should be doing and what we shouldn't.

- Knowing what we are to own and take responsibility for gives us freedom. If each of us knows where our yard begins and ends, we are free to do with it what we like.

- Boundaries do more than just allow us to care for ourselves. They also help us care for others in a healthy way.

- Maintaining boundaries — or, put differently, taking responsibility for our life — opens up many different options.

Realizing that we don't need to be limited by circumstances, other people, or the dictates of a critical inner voice, we can take greater control of our time, energy, and resources and experience the freedom of doing whatever we want and serving others in the ways we choose.

- The freedom that comes with knowing our own boundaries leads to love because love requires freedom. If we feel free to say no, then when we choose to give, we are giving out of love, and our service is truly Christlike.

- We need to take responsibility for our feelings, attitudes, beliefs, behaviors, choices, thoughts, values, limits, talents, desires, and love.

Praying Together

Having heard that helpful and challenging summary of today's lesson, let's close in prayer:

God, you know us and you know where our lives resemble Sherrie's—where we have failed to establish boundaries, where we have failed to build gates in our fences, and where we are keeping out good and keeping in bad. You also know the reasons for all that—the past hurts, the poor models, the misunderstood teachings. But we want to establish healthy boundaries. Teach us to take responsibility for our feelings, attitudes, beliefs, behaviors, choices, values, limits, talents, thoughts, desires, and love. Help us learn to establish appropriate boundaries so that we may experience healthy relationships, love, and freedom. We pray in Jesus' name, Amen.

Suggested Reading

For more thoughts on this session's topic, read chapters 1 and 2 in the book *Boundaries:* "A Day in a Boundaryless Life" and "What Does a Boundary Look Like?"

Understanding Boundaries

*I*n this session you will:

- Identify specific struggles in establishing and enforcing boundaries
- Determine how boundary problems develop and how boundaries are injured

Exploring Together

Boundary Problems

In the first session, we acknowledged that each of us needs to take responsibility for what is within our boundaries — our feelings, our attitudes and beliefs, our behaviors, our choices, our thoughts and values, our limits, our talents, our desires, and our love. That's hard work!

And it's harder for some of us than others because of certain boundary problems. These problems come in a variety of recognizable patterns, and you may see yourself in one or more of these descriptions:

- *Compliants* say yes to bad things because they haven't learned how to say no or even that it's okay to say no to the bad.

- *Avoidants* say no to the good. They aren't able to ask for help; their boundaries keep people — and often even God — out. Needs, problems, and even legitimate wants seem bad and destructive.

- *Controllers* hear no as simply a challenge to change the other person's mind. Controllers can't respect other people's limits.

- *Nonresponsives* neglect the responsibilities of love by not responding to other people's needs.

- Boundary problems also arise when we can't distinguish between *functional boundaries* (these involve the ability to complete a task, project, or job) and *relational boundaries* (these involve the ability to speak truth to those with whom we are in relationship).

Talking Together

Diagnosing Boundary Problems

You may find it easier to diagnose someone else rather than yourself, so take a look at the following six scenarios. Make your diagnosis of the person whose name appears in bold—compliant, avoidant, controller, nonresponsive, or a combination of these categories—and answer the questions that follow.

Scenario #1

Marti had begun to see a pattern in her life. In her words, "When someone needs four hours with me, I can't say no. But when I need someone for ten minutes, I can't ask for that. Isn't there a computer chip in my head I can replace?"

Diagnosis: _____

- When is Marti compliant? When is she avoidant?

- Why would this cycle be draining?

- What problems might being a compliant avoidant cause in marriage? parenting? the workplace? relationships?

Scenario #2

Brenda and **Mike** were talking in their bedroom after putting the kids to bed. Brenda began to unburden her fears about childrearing and her feelings of inadequacy at work. Without warning, Mike turned to her and said, "If you don't like the way you feel, change your feelings. Life's tough. So just ... just handle it, Brenda."

Diagnosis: _____

- What is the difference between being responsible *for* another person and responsible *to* another person? Which is healthy? Why?

- Explain why nonresponsiveness is often expressed with criticism and has its roots in narcissism.

- What problems might Mike's nonresponsiveness cause in his marriage? his parenting? the workplace?

Scenario #3

Robert was the only boy in his family, the youngest of four children. His sisters were three to seven years older than he was. Until he was in the sixth grade, they were bigger and stronger, and they would beat him until he was bruised. His parents said, "Boys don't hit girls. It's bad manners." He was triple teamed, but was told that fighting back—protecting himself—was unacceptable.

Diagnosis: _____

- What were Robert's parents teaching him about boundaries? (What did your parents teach you with their words and actions?)

- Why do some people say yes to bad things?

- What problems might Robert's compliance cause in his marriage? his parenting? the workplace?

Scenario #4

"What do you mean, you're quitting? You can't leave now!" **Steve** looked at Frank, his administrative assistant for several years. Frank had given his all, even spending unpaid vacation time at the office on projects and switching his vacation schedule twice at Steve's insistence. The final straw came when Steve began calling Frank at home almost every day during dinnertime. Several times Frank had tried to talk with Steve about the time violations, but Steve never really understood. After all, he needed Frank: Frank made him look successful.

Diagnosis: _Controller (Steve)_

- What responsibility is Steve avoiding?

  — Steve won't take ownership of his own responsibilities
  — Steve doesn't listen well

- In what ways is Steve being controlling through the use of aggression? manipulation?

- What problems might Steve's control cause in his marriage? his parenting? the workplace? his relationships?

Scenario #5

Tonight the five couples who had been meeting together for six months suddenly became more intimate. The sharing went beyond the usual "please pray for Aunt Sarah" requests to the real struggles in their lives. When people asked their host, **Rachel**, to share, she cleared her throat and finally spoke: "After hearing all the other problems, I don't think my issues are anything compared to what you all deal with. So ... who'd like dessert?"

Diagnosis: _Avoidance_

- What has Rachel learned about boundaries? What has she learned about her problems and probably about her God-given needs?

  She can't recognize her own needs

- What problems arise when boundaries function more like walls than fences?

  Keep the good out ; keep the bad in

- What problems might Rachel's avoidance cause in her marriage? her parenting? the workplace? her relationships? her relationship with God?

Scenario #6

Brad hung up the phone after talking to **Brenda**, his mom. Brad and his wife, Allison, had made plans for a much-needed getaway as a couple, but the date happened to fall on Brenda's birthday. When Brenda heard about the plans, she called Brad and complained to him about how selfish he was being and how lonely he was making her. When he tried to explain that their plans weren't directed against her and that he and Allison really needed the break, Brenda refused to listen to Brad's needs and concerns for his marriage. The couple scuttled their plans and resignedly prepared for a trip to Mom's.

Diagnosis: _____

- How is Brenda both nonresponsive and controlling at the same time?

- Why would a controlling nonresponsive be attracted to a compliant avoidant?

- What problems might being a controlling nonresponsive — like Brenda — cause in marriage? parenting? the workplace? relationships?

Boundary Building ... On Your Own

For You to Do After This Session and Before the Next One

1. In which quadrant of the "Summary of Boundary Problems" chart below do you see yourself? You may find yourself in more than one. In which quadrants would you categorize the one or two people with whom you are struggling most today?

Summary of Boundary Problems

	CAN'T SAY	CAN'T HEAR
NO	The compliant feels guilty and/or controlled by others; can't set boundaries	The controller aggressively or manipulatively violates boundaries of others
YES	The nonresponsive sets boundaries against responsibility to love	The avoidant sets boundaries against receiving care from others

2. Do you have good functional boundaries but poor relational boundaries? Or do you have good relational boundaries but poor functional boundaries? Why do you think your boundary strengths and weaknesses are what they are?

Exploring Together

A Handful of Facts

We've looked at some boundary problems. Now let's consider how boundaries develop. The family in which you grew up has a lot to do with whether or not you have healthy boundaries today.

- First, boundaries aren't inherited; they're built. Boundary development is an ongoing process, and its most crucial stages are in our very early years.

- The Scriptures advise parents to "train a child in the way he should go, and when he is old he will not turn from it" (Prov. 22:6). This verse calls parents to train their children in the way God has planned for them to go. Good parenting is being a partner in helping young ones discover what God intends them to be and helping them reach that goal.

- Boundaries develop in distinct phases (as you'll hear about on the DVD).

- Foundational to healthy boundary development are supportive relationships with God and other people. Don't even try to start setting limits until you have entered into deep, abiding attachments with people who will love you no matter what.

- We human beings are built for relationships and attachment to one another. Attachment to other human beings is the foundation of our existence. When this foundation is cracked or faulty, boundaries are impossible to develop because, when we lack relationship, we have nowhere to go in a conflict. Furthermore, when we aren't secure that we are loved, we are forced to choose between two bad options: setting limits at the risk of losing a relationship or not setting limits and remaining a prisoner to the wishes of another person.

Learning Together

DVD Segment: "Boundary Development and Obstacles to It"

Now Dr. Cloud will talk about boundary development and identify some hindrances to the development of healthy boundaries.

- Boundaries develop as a normal part of our interaction with our families.

- The first developmental task of infants is to bond with their mom and dad. They need to learn that they are welcome and safe in the world.

- Healthy bonding leads to healthy separation and individualism. The baby's need for autonomy, or independence, starts to emerge.

- Hatching, practicing, and rapprochement are three additional phases critical to the development of healthy boundaries.

- Two additional periods later in life also focus on boundaries. The first is adolescence. The adolescent years are in some ways similar to the first few years of life. They involve more mature issues, such as sexuality, gender identity, competition, and adult identity, but the same issues of knowing when to say yes and no—and to whom—are central during this confusing time.

- The second period is young adulthood, the time when children leave home or college and start a career or get married. During this period young adults suffer a loss of structure and experience new demands of intimacy and commitment. This can be an intense time of learning more about setting good boundaries.

- The process of healthy boundary development can be interrupted by a variety of things—withdrawal of love when boundaries are exercised, hostility against boundaries, overcontrol, a lack of limits, inconsistent limits, trauma (or abuse), character traits, and sinfulness.

Talking Together

A Biblical View of Healthy Boundary Development

Scripture offers great insight into what needs to happen in each phase of development and why each of these phases is crucial to the establishment of healthy boundaries.

Bonding or connecting with their parents gives infants a sense of safety and security.

1. In Genesis 2:18, what observation about human beings does God make?

2. What phrases from Ephesians 3:17 and Colossians 2:7 refer to this kind of emotional object constancy?

Separation refers to a child's need to perceive of him- or herself as distinct from Mother, a "not me" experience. **Individuation** describes the identity children develop while separating from Mother, a "me" experience. You can't have "me" until you have "not me." An individual must first determine who he or she isn't before discovering the true authentic aspects of his or her God-given identity.

3. Look at young Jesus in Luke 2:41–49. What evidence of separation do you see here? What evidence of individuation do you see?

Hatching occurs between five and ten months of age as infants move from "Mommy and I are the same" to "Mommy and I aren't the same."

Practicing children are those who are trying to leave Mom. Their newfound ability to walk opens up a sense of omnipotence. In this phase, children learn that aggressiveness and taking initiative are good.

Rapprochement, which occurs from around eighteen months to three years, is that phase when the grandiosity of the past few months slowly gives way to the realization that "I can't do everything I want." This phase is a return to connection with Mother.

4. In Matthew 5:37 Jesus calls us to let our yes be yes and our no be no. Why and when is it important for our children to be able to say no?

5. What does the warning of Proverbs 19:18 say about the importance of helping children learn to accept limits when they encounter a no?

Boundary Building ... On Your Own

For You to Do After This Session and Before the Next One

1. What attitude toward boundaries was modeled in the home in which you grew up? Be specific.

2. How have your boundaries been injured? See the last bullet point in "Learning Together: Boundary Development and Obstacles to It" (page 35) for a list of things that can interrupt healthy boundary development.

Praying Together

This session's discussion of boundary problems and boundary development has undoubtedly given you important insight into yourself. So let's spend a few minutes in prayer, thanking God for what we've learned, asking for healing where we need it, and requesting his help in our boundary-building efforts.

Lord, thank you for the glimpse we've had into who you've created us to be and how you intend healthy boundaries to develop. We don't yet have the healthy boundaries you want us to have. Thank you that you can heal the hurts caused by boundaries not honored or boundaries not maintained—and that you will help us build healthy boundaries as we seek your guidance. In Jesus' name, Amen.

Suggested Reading

For more thoughts on this session's topic, read chapters 3 and 4 in the book *Boundaries*: "Boundary Problems" and "How Boundaries Are Developed."

The Laws of Boundaries, Part I

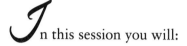n this session you will:

- Discover what the Bible says about how boundaries should operate in our lives
- Learn how boundaries can be developed throughout our lives

Learning Together

DVD Segment #1: "Lessons in the Laws of Boundaries"

Last time we met, we looked at categories of boundary problems — at compliants, who say yes to bad; avoidants, who say no to good; controllers, who don't respect other people's limits; and nonresponsives, who don't respond to other people's needs. These problems occur when the process of healthy boundary development is interrupted. Now, during this session and the next, we'll look at what the Bible says about how boundaries should operate in our lives and how we can develop them throughout our lives. Let's begin with a short DVD presentation.

- People raised in families where God's ways of boundaries are not practiced never know the principles that could have helped them operate in accord with reality instead of against it.

- The reality God has established is an orderly one based on knowable laws and principles. These spiritual realities are as real as gravity.

- Law #1 is the Law of Sowing and Reaping. This law of cause and effect is a basic law of life. When God tells us in Galatians 6:7 – 8 that we will reap what we sow, he is not punishing us; he's telling us how things really are.

- Law #2 is the Law of Responsibility, which includes loving others (John 15:12; Gal. 5:13 – 14). In fact, anytime you are not loving others, you are not taking full responsibility for yourself; you have disowned your heart. We are to *love* one another, not *be* one another. You are responsible for yourself. I am responsible for myself (Phil. 2:12 – 13).

Talking Together

Lessons in the Laws of Boundaries

The Law of Sowing and Reaping and the Law of Responsibility are the first two of the ten Laws of Boundaries. Let's consider together how these first two laws of boundaries function in our life each and every day.

Law #1: The Law of Sowing and Reaping

1. What are some effects (the reaping) of certain everyday behaviors (the sowing)? Consider negatives (overeating, overspending, selfishness, ignoring Gods commandments, etc.) as well as positives (eating right, exercising regularly, budgeting wisely, etc.). Be sure to discuss the consequences (reaping) of enforcing or failing to enforce boundaries (sowing).

2. Give three examples of how or when parents interrupt the Law of Sowing and Reaping (Gal. 6:7–8) in their children's lives. What, for instance, has happened to the person who says, "I can't discipline my spending because I was never taught to save"?

3. We call a person who continually rescues or enables another person to be an irresponsible "codependent." What are some reasons why codependent people have a hard time allowing others to suffer consequences?

4. Why are consequences more effective teachers than confrontations?

Boundary Building ... On Your Own

For You to Do After This Session and Before the Next One

1. Give an example of positive and negative sowing in your life. In each case, what did you reap? What are you sowing now?

2. When have consequences for your actions prompted you to make some changes?

3. Where do you need to stop interrupting the Law of Sowing and Reaping in someone's life?

Law #2: The Law of Responsibility

1. What would you say to someone who asked, "Create my own boundaries? Isn't that awfully selfish?"

2. Taking responsibility for one's life includes loving others (John 15:12). What does it mean that we are to *love* one another, not *be* one another?

3. Read Philippians 2:12–13. Explain the difference between being responsible *to* and being responsible *for*.

4. One aspect of being responsible to someone is setting limits on that person's destructive and irresponsible behavior. Why would rescuing that person from the consequences of his or her destructive behavior be irresponsible?

Boundary Building ... On Your Own

For You to Do After This Session and Before the Next One

1. What are you doing to take responsibility for your personal and spiritual growth?

2. Where are you trying to take responsibility for someone else's personal and spiritual growth?

3. When have you been hurt — or when have you hurt someone — because limits were not put on a certain behavior?

4. What behavior currently affecting you, if any, do you need to put limits on?

Learning Together

DVD Segment #2: "More Lessons in the Laws of Boundaries"

We've covered the first two laws. Now let's look at the next three.

- Law #3 is the Law of Power. The words of the apostle Paul in Romans 7:15–23 reveal the powerlessness of us human beings over our addictions, our unhealthy patterns, and our sinful ways. Though you do not have the power in and of yourself to overcome your sinful patterns, you do have the power to do some things that will bring fruits of victory later. Law #3 identifies those powers.

  1. You have the power to agree with the truth about your problems (confession).
  2. You have the power to submit your inability to God and turn your life over to him. He can do what you are unable to do: bring about change (Matt. 5:3, 6; James 4:7–10; 1 John 1:9).
  3. You have the power to ask God and others to reveal more and more about what is within your boundaries.

4. You have the power to turn from the evil that you find within you (repentance).
5. You have the power to humble yourself and ask God and others to help you with your developmental injuries and leftover childhood needs.
6. You have the power to seek out those whom you have injured and make amends.
7. You have the power to forgive those who have hurt you.

- Law #4 is the Law of Respect. We need to respect the boundaries of others in order to earn respect for our own. We need to treat their boundaries the way we want them to treat ours. It's the Golden Rule of Matthew 7:12 where Jesus said, "So in everything, do to others what you would have them do to you." We need to respect other people's boundaries. When we accept their freedom (including their freedom to say no), we don't get angry, feel guilty, or withdraw our love when they set boundaries with us. When we walk in the Spirit and accept others' freedom, we also are free (2 Cor. 3:17).

- Law #5, the Law of Motivation, says, "Freedom first, service second." In Matthew 20:26, Jesus calls us to serve, and he modeled a life of service when he walked this earth. But many people serve because they fear that they will lose love or that people will be angry with them if they don't serve. If people serve out of these or any other false motives, they are doomed to failure. If people serve freely out of gratitude, an overflowing heart, and love for others, they realize that it truly is more blessed to give than to receive (Acts 20:35). The Law of Motivation calls us to give bountifully and freely out of a heart of gratitude rather than a heart of fear.

Don't get guilted into serving others.

Talking Together

More Lessons in the Laws of Boundaries

Law #3 talks about what we have power over. Law #4 calls us to respect other people's boundaries. Law #5 points out ways in which fear and guilt keep us from serving freely from a heart full of gratitude and love. These three laws will become more real to us when we think about them in terms of our own lives. Let's do exactly that as we answer the following questions.

Law #3: The Law of Power

1. Read what Paul says in Romans 7:15–23. What phrases can you especially identify with? When have you felt this kind of powerlessness? Be specific about the sin, unhealthy habit, or addiction.

2. What powers listed on pages 44–45 surprise you? encourage you? intimidate you?

3. Explain why these powers to do certain specific things will bring fruits of victory later.

Law #4: The Law of Respect

1. In Matthew 7:12 Jesus said, "So in everything, do to others what you would have them do to you." In light of this command, what can you do to show respect for someone's boundaries?

2. Explain why our acceptance of other people's freedom to set their own boundaries is freeing for us.

3. Why would someone's respect for your boundaries be empowering?

Law #5: The Law of Motivation

1. Jesus calls us to serve (Matt. 20:26). But many people serve out of guilt or because they fear that they will lose love or that people will be angry with them if they don't serve. Other false motives for serving are: attempting to avoid loneliness; thinking that to love means always saying yes; thinking that "good" people always say yes; trying to overcome the guilt inside and feel good about themselves; paying back all that they have received; trying to gain people's approval (especially people who represent their parents whose approval was withheld); and overidentifying with the other's loss and feeling the sadness they think their no would cause. What life experiences and early relationships can help engender false motives for service? Give two or three examples.

2. When have you experienced that it truly is more blessed to give than to receive (Acts 20:35)? Be specific about the circumstances and your feelings.

Boundary Building ... On Your Own

For You to Do After This Session and Before the Next One

Law #3: The Law of Power

1. What powers listed on pages 44–45 do you need to begin exercising in your life?

2. What is the first step you will take—today—to exercise one of the powers you just listed? Whom will you ask to help you?

Law #4: The Law of Respect

1. With whom have you been caught up in a fear cycle and therefore been afraid to set the boundaries you need to set? With whom do you comply rather than set boundaries?

2. Whose boundaries do you need to have more respect for? To whom do you need to grant the freedom to be him- or herself and different from you (2 Cor. 3:17)?

Law #5: The Law of Motivation

1. Which, if any, of your "doing" and sacrificing are motivated not by love, but by fear that you won't be loved or fear of anger if you don't comply?

2. What step will you take to deal with your fear, guilt, or other false motives for serving?

Praying Together

The Laws of Sowing and Reaping, of Responsibility, of Power, of Respect, and of Motivation—we've covered a lot of territory. Let's close our time together by asking God to help us live according to these principles.

Thank you, Father, that the reality you established is based on knowable laws and principles. Thank you for this opportunity to learn about spiritual laws that are as real as the physical laws of gravity and entropy. Help us learn to live according to your life-giving principles. We pray in Jesus' name, Amen.

Suggested Reading

For more thoughts on this session's topic,
read the first half of chapter 5 (through Law #5) in the book
Boundaries: "Ten Laws of Boundaries."

The Laws of Boundaries, Part II

*I*n this session you will:

- Discover more about what the Bible says about how boundaries should operate in our lives
- Learn further how boundaries can be developed throughout life

Learning Together

DVD Segment #1: "Laws #6 and #7"

Last time we met, we talked about how the Laws of Boundaries give us freedom, and we looked at the first five laws.

■ ■ ■

The Law of Sowing and Reaping teaches that we can learn from the consequences of our decisions as long as no one interrupts the cause-and-effect process.

The Law of Responsibility calls us to take responsibility for our life, and that responsibility includes loving other people.

The Law of Power identifies the power we have to do certain things.

The Law of Respect encourages us to respect the boundaries of others in order to earn respect for our own.

The Law of Motivation says, "Freedom first, service second." It's a call to move beyond serving because we fear losing love or having people angry at us; it's a call to serve out of gratitude.

■ ■ ■

During this lesson, we'll look at what the Bible says about how the five remaining Laws of Boundaries should operate in our lives and how we can develop boundaries throughout life.

- Things can hurt us but not harm us. In fact, things that hurt can even be good for us—and things that feel good can be very harmful to us.

- Law #6 is the Law of Evaluation. We need to evaluate the effects of setting boundaries and being responsible to the other person, but that does not mean we should avoid setting boundaries because someone might respond with hurt or anger.

- Just as iron sharpens iron (Prov. 27:17), we need confrontation and truth from others to grow. None of us likes to hear negative things about ourselves, but in the long run, hearing those things may be good for us (Prov. 27:6; Eph. 4:25).

- We need to evaluate the painful effects caused by setting boundaries and by the confrontations that come with enforcing those boundaries, and we need to see how that hurt is helpful.

- Law #7 is the Law of Proactivity. Just as in the physical world, in the spiritual realm of human relationships, for every action, there is an equal and opposite reaction (Rom. 4:15; 5:20; 7:5; Eph. 6:4; Col. 3:21). After years of compliance, for instance, a person's pent-up rage may explode. Reactive phases like that are necessary for the establishment of boundaries, but not sufficient.

- Proactive people show what they love, what they want, what they purpose, and what they stand for — as opposed to those who are known by what they hate, what they don't like, what they stand against, and what they will not do. Proactive people are able to "love others as themselves," "die to self," and not "return evil for evil."

Talking Together

Laws #6 and #7

Once again, talking about these laws will help us better understand them and better live out the lessons they teach us.

Law #6: The Law of Evaluation

1. Explain the difference between hurting and harming someone.

2. What kinds of healthy boundaries may cause pain to other people? Give two or three specific examples.

3. When has someone protected his or her boundaries and done something that hurt you? Did that action harm you? Explain.

Boundary Building ... On Your Own

For You to Do After This Session and Before the Next One

1. What current circumstances call for you to set boundaries?

2. If you set boundaries, what pain or disappointment might you cause someone you love? Will that pain harm the person?

Law #7: The Law of Proactivity

1. What are the benefits of reactive phases, those stages when people react against oppression, victimization, emotional blackmail, manipulation, and other abusive situations?

2. Why must such reactive phases necessarily be limited? Consider what Paul says in Galatians 5:13, 15.

3. Proactive people show what they love, what they want, what they purpose, and what they stand for—as opposed to those who are known by what they hate, what they don't like, what they stand against, and what they will not do. What benefits come with being proactive? Give a few real-life examples.

Boundary Building ... On Your Own

For You to Do After This Session and Before the Next One

1. Where are you on the continuum between proactive and reactive as described in question #3 above?

2. In what relationship(s) is it time for you to move past the reactive to the proactive and begin living out of the power of love? What steps will you take toward that end?

Learning Together

DVD Segment #2: "Laws #8, #9, and #10"

We're almost through the ten Laws of Boundaries. Right now Dr. Cloud will walk us through the final three.

- Law #8 is the Law of Envy. Boundaryless people feel empty and unfulfilled. They look at another's sense of fullness and feel envious (Gal. 6:4). That time and energy need to be spent on taking responsibility for their lack and doing something about it.

- Envy should always be a sign to us that we are lacking something. At that moment, we need to ask God to help us understand what we resent, why we do not have whatever we are envying, and whether we truly need it. We should ask him either to show us how to get there or to help us grieve what we cannot have and be content with what we do have.

- Law #9 is the Law of Activity. Many times we have boundary problems because we lack initiative—the God-given ability to propel ourselves into life. God wants us to be assertive and active, seeking and knocking on the door of life. The sin that God rebukes is not trying and failing, but failing to try (Luke 19:12–27). "Just do it!" should be more than a tennis shoe advertisement! Trying, failing, and trying again is called learning.

- Evil is an active force, and passivity can become an ally of evil by not pushing against it. That is the role of boundaries: they define and preserve our property, our self. And our boundaries can be created only by our being active and aggressive, by our knocking, seeking, and asking. So we need to move out of passivity by taking initiative to set healthy boundaries.

- Law #10 is the Law of Exposure. As we've said in this series, a boundary defines where an individual begins and ends. The Law of Exposure says that our boundaries need to be made visible to others and communicated to them in relationships (Eph. 4:25–26; 5:13–14).

- We have many boundary problems because of relational fears—fears of guilt, of not being liked, of the loss of love, loss of connection, loss of approval, of receiving anger, of being known, and so on. These relational problems can be solved only in relationships, for that is the context of the problems themselves.

- The Law of Exposure acknowledges that our boundaries are affected by sin and that boundaries need to be brought into the light for God to heal them and for others to benefit from them. This is the path to real love: openly communicating your boundaries.

Talking Together

Laws #8, #9, and #10

The truths that Dr. Cloud just explained are exciting and empowering. Let's take a couple steps toward applying those truths to our lives.

Law #8: The Law of Envy

1. What things and what people do you tend to envy most? What does your answer show you about yourself?

2. What step will you take toward getting what you lack? What might God be calling you to do about that lack?

Law #9: The Law of Activity

1. How easy or difficult is it for you to take initiative in life? When have you seen—in someone's life or perhaps your own—passivity become an ally of evil by not pushing against it? Also, in what aspect of your life are you failing to try right now?

2. As a result of this discussion, what do you think you could
   or should be pursuing more actively? Where will you begin to
   knock, seek, and ask? Be specific. What baby step will you take
   to begin exercising your "initiative muscle"?

Law #10: The Law of Exposure

1. With whom do you struggle to communicate your boundaries?
   Why? What aspects of yourself do you hide? Why?

2. With which safe person in your life will you begin to share the
   hidden parts of yourself? With whom will you start trying to
   communicate your boundaries? If appropriate, ask God to bring
   into your life someone safe with whom you can gradually begin
   to both share all of yourself and communicate openly.

Learning Together

DVD Segment #3: "What We've Learned"

We've now looked at all ten Laws of Boundaries. Whatever you're feeling—overwhelmed, empowered, excited about getting to work on boundaries, unsure of where to start—hear this word of encouragement:

Each of us *can* learn from God's Word the principles for healthy boundaries. We can also rely on his guidance and his Spirit to help us fight the battles that will occur as we strive to make God's ways part of our character. God has brought us out from an alien land, and he is teaching us his ways.

Praying Together

It's good to know that we're not in the boundary-building business alone—that God himself will guide us and his Holy Spirit will empower us. Let's pray.

Father, thank you for teaching us about your laws for relationships, laws that you designed for our well-being. Thank you for what you've shown us about how these laws are rooted in your truth and your love. As we continue to learn your laws, we ask you to help us practice them, internalize them, and ultimately find freedom in them. We pray in Jesus' name, Amen.

Suggested Reading

For more thoughts on this session's topic, read the second half of chapter 5 (from Law #6 onward) in the book *Boundaries*: "Ten Laws of Boundaries."

Myths about Boundaries

*I*n this session you will:

- Look at eight myths about boundaries
- Investigate which myths about boundaries you have accepted as truth
- Learn what you can do to get free of those myths that entangle and ensnare you

Learning Together

DVD Segment: "Myths about Boundaries"

In the past two sessions, we looked at the ten Laws of Boundaries. Today we're going to look at eight myths about boundaries. One definition of *myth* is "a fiction that looks like a truth," and many myths have grown up around boundaries. Let's hear what Dr. Townsend and Dr. Cloud have to say.

- *Myth #1: If I set boundaries, I'm being selfish.* Boundaries don't turn us from other-centeredness to self-centeredness. Instead, boundaries actually increase our ability to care about others.

- *Myth #2: Boundaries are a sign of disobedience.* In reality, a lack of boundaries is often a sign of disobedience. We must establish boundaries because, among other reasons, if we can't say no, we can't say yes.

- *Myth #3: If I begin setting boundaries, I will be hurt by others.* Boundaries are a litmus test of the quality of our relationships. Those people in our lives who can respect our boundaries will love our wills, our opinions, our separateness.

- *Myth #4: If I set boundaries, I will hurt others.* Boundaries are not an offensive weapon, but a defensive tool. They simply prevent our treasures from being taken at the wrong time.

- *Myth #5: Boundaries mean I am angry.* Boundaries themselves don't cause anger in us. But anger is a sign that our boundaries have been violated, that we don't have boundaries, or that we need to confront the threat. Anger also provides us with a sense of power to solve a problem.

- *Myth #6: When others set boundaries, it injures me.* If we want others to respect our boundaries, then we must be willing to respect the boundaries of others.

- *Myth #7: Boundaries cause feelings of guilt.* God doesn't allow the issues of gratitude and boundaries to be confused, and neither should we. Our feelings of gratitude need not obligate us to fail to set boundaries with those who have given gifts to us.

- *Myth #8: Boundaries are permanent, and I'm afraid of burning my bridges.* It's important to understand that your no is always subject to you. You own your boundaries; they don't own you. You can renegotiate or change a boundary when you are in a safer place.

Talking Together

Debunking the Myths

The questions we'll discuss now will help us sort through the information in the DVD and see what it means for each one of us.

Myth #1: If I set boundaries, I'm being selfish.

1. Explain why setting healthy boundaries is a matter of healthy stewardship of the life God has given us — and not ungodly selfishness.

2. What do verses like Matthew 7:7, Matthew 25:13, 2 Corinthians 5:10, and Philippians 2:12–13 suggest about what we are responsible for?

3. Why do appropriate boundaries actually increase our ability to care about others? Give two or three specific examples.

Boundary Building ... On Your Own

For You to Do After This Session and Before the Next One

In what current relationship would clearer, stronger boundaries enable you to be a stronger, more caring participant?

Myth #2: Boundaries are a sign of disobedience.

1. In 2 Corinthians 9:7 we read about the attitude of obedience that pleases God. What does this verse suggest about those times when we say yes but mean no? An internal no nullifies an external yes (Hos. 6:6).

2. While we find ourselves living under various authorities, our disobedience to them is ultimately disobedience to God. Give an example of when a lack of boundaries can be a sign of such disobedience. Hint: Consider saying no to good things for the wrong reasons.

Boundary Building ... On Your Own

For You to Do After This Session and Before the Next One

1. Reflect on a commitment you made with an external yes despite your internal no. Did you fulfill that commitment? If so, with what attitude?

2. Where are you currently acting out of fear — "reluctantly" and "under compulsion" (2 Cor. 9:7) — rather than out of love (1 John 4:18)?

Myth #3: If I begin setting boundaries, I will be hurt by others.

1. Why are boundaries a litmus test for the quality of our relationships? What do we learn when a person has trouble respecting our boundaries and accepting our no, when a person seems to love us only when we say yes (Luke 6:26)?

2. The Bible clearly distinguishes between those who love truth (the "wise" and "righteous") and those who don't (Prov. 10:23; Phil. 4:8). In what ways is setting limits or establishing boundaries akin to telling the truth? Consider the fact that God is more concerned about our heart than our outward compliance.

3. Why might people close to us be threatened when we establish boundaries? What role can safe places of being "rooted and grounded in love" (Eph. 3:17 NASB) play as a person learns to tell the truth?

Boundary Building ... On Your Own

For You to Do After This Session and Before the Next One

1. Setting boundaries is a way to tell the truth about who you are. When has your setting boundaries led to increased intimacy in a relationship?

2. Consider in what relationship you need to establish some boundaries today. What do you feel the risks are? When will you take the bold step of setting limits? Who will be there to support you with prayer?

Myth #4: If I set boundaries, I will hurt others.

1. Explain what is meant by the statement, "Boundaries are a defensive tool rather than an offensive weapon." Consider Proverbs 4:23.

2. Some people fear that they will hurt others by establishing and maintaining boundaries because they project their own wounded or sad parts onto those other people and overidentify with those people's perhaps nonexistent pain. These fearful people feel that if they have limits, they are not being loving and are in fact being hurtful. When has your concern that your no would hurt someone kept you from establishing or maintaining boundaries? What feelings and experiences do you think lay behind your concern?

3. Why is it important to have a group of supportive relationships? What can happen if you are relying on God and just one best friend? When we've taken the responsibility to develop several supportive relationships in a biblical fashion (Eph. 4:2–3), why are we better able to handle someone's no?

Boundary Building ... On Your Own

For You to Do After This Session and Before the Next One

There are times when, for some reason or another, people can't sacrifice and help us even when our needs are legitimate. In light of this truth, how do you want to respond — internally and externally — the next time someone maintains appropriate boundaries and leaves you to look elsewhere to get your needs met?

Myth #5: Boundaries mean I am angry.

1. Explore why beginning to set limits might put you in touch with some feelings of old anger. Then explain how anger — which signals that our boundaries have been violated and which provides us with a sense of power to solve a problem — can be an ally. (Look at Jesus in John 2:13 – 17.)

2. It takes years to dissipate anger stemming from years of no's that were never voiced, never listened to, never respected. Why does establishing boundaries decrease and even prevent some anger? Consider the "early warning system" function of anger.

Boundary Building ... On Your Own

For You to Do After This Session and Before the Next One

1. Do you let yourself experience anger? Why or why not? If you do, how do you deal with it?

2. When has anger energized you to confront someone or set a limit? Be specific about what you were protecting or what problem you were solving.

3. Are you aware of "old anger" still inside your heart? If so, what are you doing to work through it appropriately? How do you want to deal with anger without sinning against someone (Eph. 4:26, 31)?

Myth #6: When others set boundaries, it injures me.

1. Why would having inappropriate boundaries set on us, especially in childhood, injure us and make it hard for us to accept people's boundaries?

2. We may be unable to accept someone's boundary if we have made that person too important. What might this unhealthy situation look like in a marriage?

3. When we have a problem accepting another person's boundary, it may be that we have a problem with taking ownership of our own responsibilities. Why would a history of being rescued lead to this kind of problem?

4. If you feel hurt by someone's boundaries—by someone saying no—what kind of old hurt could be behind your present pain? What could a person do to resolve that kind of pain?

5. Read what Jesus says in Matthew 7:12. What does this rule say to you about boundaries?

Boundary Building ... On Your Own

For You to Do After This Session and Before the Next One

When Paul set limits on the Corinthians' rebelliousness, they responded with sorrow and repentance (2 Cor. 7:8–9). Describe a situation in your world where setting boundaries—either your setting boundaries for yourself or someone maintaining boundaries in their relationship with you—might lead to repentance.

Myth #7: Boundaries cause feelings of guilt.

1. One of the major obstacles to setting boundaries with people in our life is our feeling of obligation: the idea that because we have received something, we owe something. God's gift of salvation cost his Son (John 3:16). What does Colossians 2:7 suggest about how we should respond to that ultimate gift—and any other gift as well? What is going on with the giver when that person gives intangible gifts (love, time, energy) without strings attached?

2. As the Revelation letters to the churches of Ephesus, Pergamum, and Thyatira illustrate, God doesn't allow validation and boundaries to be confused. Although he validates the churches and praises their accomplishments for the kingdom, he does set boundaries with them by confronting their irresponsibilities (Rev. 2:4, 14, 20). Why aren't validation and boundaries mutually exclusive? Why are they so easily confused and interwoven?

Boundary Building … On Your Own

For You to Do After This Session and Before the Next One

1. When have feelings of obligation prevented you from setting boundaries? What were the consequences of your failure to set boundaries? Are you, for instance, stuck at home, in school, church, a job, or a friendship?

2. What relationship is God calling you to set boundaries in, despite what that person has given you?

**Myth #8: Boundaries are permanent,
and I'm afraid of burning my bridges.**

1. The Bible shows us many instances when boundaries were
   renegotiated and changed (Jonah 3:10 and Acts 15:37–39,
   together with 2 Tim. 4:11). Boundaries—which you can always
   change—can help preserve a relationship, and temporary
   boundaries can bring people back together. Give at least one
   example of each of these situations.

2. Why is it important to recognize the difference between owning
   our boundaries and being owned by them? Which option gives
   power and freedom to grow? Explain.

Boundary Building ... On Your Own

For You to Do After This Session and Before the Next One

1. What boundaries have you failed to set due to your fear that
   they would be permanent?

2. What boundaries are you more willing to set knowing that they
   needn't be permanent?

Boundary Building ... On Your Own

For You to Do After This Session and Before the Next One

"Reflections"

Spend a few minutes thinking about the eight myths in a more personal way.

1. Up to this point, what has been your greatest fear about setting boundaries? How, if at all, have the truths discussed in this session eased that fear?

2. Where in your life right now do you most need to establish boundaries? What have you determined to do as a result of what you've learned in this session about God's truth, boundaries, and yourself?

Praying Together

Whatever you're feeling — overwhelmed, empowered, excited about getting to work on boundaries, unsure of where to start — be encouraged as we pray:

Lord, you have promised that your truth shall set us free, and we thank you for the truths explained in this session. Please use those truths to change us and to free us from false thinking. Guide our actions as you continue to teach us how to set boundaries wisely and how to maintain them with love. In Jesus' name, Amen.

Suggested Reading

For more thoughts on this session's topic, read chapter 6 in *Boundaries*: "Common Boundary Myths."

Boundary Conflicts, Part I

*I*n this session you will:

- Look at some potential boundary conflicts within yourself and between you and God
- Determine what healthy action you can take to avoid or deal with these potential boundary conflicts

Learning Together

DVD Segment: "Boundary Conflicts, Part I"

Last time we looked at eight common myths about boundaries, eight "sound-like-truths" that aren't true at all. We learned some powerful truths about boundaries and are therefore better able to establish and enforce our boundaries. Now, in this session we're going to look at potential conflicts within yourself and potential conflicts between you and God. You will have an opportunity to determine what healthy action you can take to avoid or deal with these conflicts.

- Here are seven common areas of internal boundary conflicts:
  1. *Eating:* Do you use food as a false boundary, to avoid intimacy by gaining weight and becoming less attractive? Do you binge, finding the comfort of food less scary than the prospect of real relationships (1 John 4:18)?
  2. *Money:* Do you struggle with impulse spending, careless budgeting, living beyond your means, credit problems, chronic borrowing from friends, ineffectual savings plans, or working more to pay all the bills? How could your love of money be the root of evil in your life (1 Tim. 6:10)?
  3. *Time management:* How do you deal with deadlines? Are you a do-ahead person or a last-minute person? How well do you manage your time (Eph. 5:16)?
  4. *Task completion:* Are you a good starter but a poor finisher (Prov. 21:5)? Have you started an exercise program, a diet, a Bible study program, or a Scripture memorization plan several times and never gotten very far?
  5. *The tongue:* Are you pleased with how often you use your tongue to bless others? Or do you use your tongue too frequently for nonstop talking, dominating conversations, gossiping, being sarcastic, threatening, flattering, or seducing (Prov. 10:19; 17:27; Matt. 12:35)?

6. *Sexuality:* Are you caught up in any out-of-control sexual behavior (Eph. 5:8 – 11)?

7. *Alcohol/substance abuse:* Are you abusing drugs and/or alcohol (1 Cor. 3:16 – 17)? Are you being honest with yourself as you evaluate your use? Are you dealing with divorce, job loss, financial havoc, or medical problems because of your use of alcohol and/or drugs?

- There are at least three reasons why our no's don't work in these seven areas:

  1. We are responsible *for* — not just *to* — the person with the problem when we are that person. We are responsible for ourselves. Simply saying no to ourselves in an attempt to establish boundaries isn't enough because of the unmet needs, unrecognized fear, or unresolved pain driving the unhealthy behavior we want to eliminate. We need to come to truly own the problem and its roots and then take responsibility for ourselves, for dealing with our unmet needs, unrecognized fear, and unresolved pain.

  2. Due to shame, fear, or our own self-sufficiency, we tend to withdraw from relationships and accountability when it comes to dealing with situations like these. Self-boundary problems worsen with increased aloneness (James 5:16).

  3. We try to use willpower to solve our boundary problems. If all we need is our will to overcome the evil within us, we certainly don't need a Savior (1 Cor. 1:17).

- We have personal boundaries in our relationship with God. He respects those boundaries — and we need to respect his.

- God respects our boundaries by leaving work for us to do that only we can do (Matt. 25:14 – 29; Phil. 2:12); by allowing us to experience the painful consequences of our behavior so that we will change and not perish (Ezek. 18:23; 2 Peter 3:9); and by respecting our no when that is our response to him (Matt. 19:16 – 22; Luke 15:11 – 24).

- God respects our boundaries, and he expects us to respect his. If we are to have a real relationship with him, we need to respect his right and freedom to say no to us. But God does not want us to be passive in our relationship with him either. In fact, he asks us to be tenacious in trying to persuade him to change his mind. Sometimes, through dialogue with us, God does change his mind (Gen. 18:16 – 33; Luke 11:5 – 9; 18:1 – 8).

- However God responds to our requests, we are to respect his wishes and stay in relationship with him.

Exploring Together

Boundary Conflicts with God

What boundary conflicts do you have with God? What boundary conflicts do you have with yourself? These are two important questions for each of us.

- When we consider boundaries and God, we need to keep in mind that relationship is what the gospel is all about. The news of Jesus Christ dying on the cross for your sins and mine is a gospel of reconciliation. Jesus' death brings hostile parties together and heals relationships between God and humanity and between people.

- Boundaries are inherent in any relationships (even our relationship with God), for boundaries define the two parties who are loving each other. Boundaries, for instance, help us see God as he really is. They enable us to negotiate life and fulfill our responsibilities. If we are trying to do God's work for him, we will fail. If we are wishing for him to do our work for us, he will refuse. But if we do our work and as God does his, we will find strength in our relationship with him.

Talking Together

Steps toward Healthy Self-Boundaries

Now let's look more closely at steps we can take toward having healthier boundaries with ourselves. We'll do that by answering several questions about three hypothetical situations:

1. Workaholism
2. An inability to maintain a relationship with a member of the opposite sex (you always do the loving; the other person, the leaving)
3. Anger that emerges at inappropriate times and in inappropriate ways

Answer the questions as if you were actually dealing with the problem and, based on those fictitious but reasonable answers, practice developing ways to resolve conflicts involving self-boundaries.

Seven Steps toward Resolving Boundary Conflicts

1. *Identify the symptoms.* What destructive fruit (depression, anxiety, panic, phobias, rage, relationship struggles, isolation, work problems, psychosomatic problems) are you experiencing because you are not able to say no to yourself?

2. *Identify the root causes of the symptoms.* Possible causes are:

- Lack of training in setting limits, in facing consequences for your actions, or in delaying gratification
- Rewarded destructiveness: learning that out-of-control behavior brings relationships
- A distortion of legitimate, God-given needs
- Fear of relationships—and your out-of-control behavior keeps people away
- A deep hunger for love that was unmet in the first few years of your life
- Being raised in a legalistic environment—and now you are rebelling
- Covering emotional hurt that came when you were neglected or abused as a child
- Emotional hurt in adult life

3. *Identify the boundary conflict.*

- Do you have weak or nonexistent boundaries in relation to eating, money, time, task completion, the tongue, sexuality, and/or alcohol and substance abuse? Ask God to help you see what areas of your life are out of control.
- Why won't sheer willpower alone work in resolving the conflict(s) you just identified?

4. *Identify who needs to take responsibility.* Your behavior pattern may be directly traceable to family problems, neglect, abuse, or trauma. Even so, explain what it means that you are responsible for your boundary conflicts.

5. *Identify what you need as you proceed along this path.* You are severely hampered in gaining either insight into or control over yourself when you are disconnected from God's people. Safe, trusting, grace-and-truth relationships are spiritual and emotional fuel. Which current relationships are giving you this fuel? Or where can you go to begin establishing such relationships?

6. *"Just do it."* How do you begin? What step do you need to take—and when will you take it? If, for instance, you missed out on your father's approval or your mother's love, which good people in your life can offer you affirmation and love now? Find such people.

Other possible steps are:

- Setting limits with safe people (begin learning assertiveness, confrontation, and honesty in a support group)
- Saying no to the bad (identify the habits or compulsions you need to renounce, repent of, and not do anymore) and forgiving the people in your life you need to forgive
- Addressing your real need (often out-of-control patterns disguise a need for something else); allowing yourself to fail (embrace and learn from failure)
- Listening to empathetic feedback from others (let people you trust provide perspective and support)
- Welcoming consequences as your teacher
- Surrounding yourself with people who are loving and supportive

Which of these steps, if any, might be good for you to take sooner rather than later?

7. *What accountability and consequences do you need to build into your program?* You might want to contract with a friend to make sure consequences happen. You could agree, for instance, that if you fall back into the unhealthy behavior, you'll pay that friend ten dollars.

Exploring Together

A Few Final Notes

Before we close our discussion of potential boundary conflicts within yourself and between you and God, consider these thoughts:

- Learning to develop mature boundaries within ourselves is not easy. Many obstacles hinder our progress; however, God desires our maturity and self-control even more than we do. He will help us and encourage us.

- Allow yourself to fail. Listen to the empathetic feedback of friends. Welcome consequences of your new behavior. Surround yourself with people who are loving and supportive.

- One last reminder: The formula we've looked at for developing self-boundaries is cyclical. That is, each time you deal with real needs, fail, get empathetic feedback, suffer consequences, and are restored, you build stronger internal boundaries. As you stay with your goal and with the right people, you will build a sense of self-restraint that can truly become part of your character for life.

Praying Together

In the next session we'll see how we can use these same principles for establishing healthy boundaries with family, friends, spouse, children, and coworkers. Right now let's ask God to help us live out what we've learned today.

God, help us see clearly when we are saying no to you—and please make us hunger and thirst for you and your righteousness. We want to have a more real relationship with you. Also teach us to respect your right to say no; to trust in your love for us, as evidenced in the Cross; and to let you be God. We thank you for inviting us to not be passive in our relationship with you, for inviting us to be persistent in prayer and tenacious in our requests. We look forward to a more real and a deeper relationship with you.

But, God, we also want to confess our out-of-control feelings and the ways they manifest themselves in our lives. Thank you that we don't need to rely on our own willpower or strength to overcome these problems. Thank you that you can help us. Open our eyes to the symptoms of our issues, their roots, and our weak or nonexistent boundaries. Help us to take ownership and learn to be responsible for ourselves—for dealing with our unmet needs, unrecognized fears, and unresolved pain. Please give us loving and supportive friends who can also help us. Give us the ability to learn from the consequences of our behaviors and the ability to receive love from friends. We pray in Jesus' name, Amen.

Suggested Reading

For more thoughts on this session's topic,
read chapters 12 and 13 in the book *Boundaries*:
"Boundaries and Your Self" and "Boundaries and God."

Session 7

Boundary Conflicts, Part II

$\mathcal{I}$n this session you will:

- Use principles you've already learned to establish boundaries with family, friends, spouse, children, and coworkers
- Discover that these five boundary conflicts are, at heart, issues of self-control rather than "other-control"

Learning Together

DVD Segment: "Boundary Conflicts, Part II"

What boundary conflicts do you have with God? What boundary conflicts do you have with yourself? These are the two important questions we looked at last time we met. Today we're going to talk about how to establish healthy boundaries with family, friends, spouse, children, and coworkers.

Each of these five areas of boundary conflicts — family, friends, spouse, children, and coworkers — is, at heart, an issue of self-control rather than "other-control."

Boundaries and Your Family

Susie made choices *on the outside*, but *on the inside* things were different. Susie and others like her do not really "own" themselves. People who own their lives do not feel guilty when they make choices. They take other people into consideration, but when they make choices for the wishes of others, they are choosing out of love, not guilt; to advance a good, not to avoid being bad.

Boundaries and Your Friends

Sean and Tim: The result of two compliants interacting is that neither does what he really wants. Each is so afraid of telling the other the truth that neither ever does.

Bill and Scott: The aggressive controller has no problem demanding or sometimes simply taking what he wants; "I need it" is enough reason for the aggressive controller to help himself to whatever the compliant has, be it car keys, a cup of sugar, or three hours.

Cathy and Sharon: Sharon is not consciously trying to manipulate her compliant friend. However, no matter what her good intentions are, when she's in a jam, Sharon uses her friends. She takes them for granted, thinking they shouldn't mind doing her a favor. Her friends go along, saying, "Well, that's just Sharon." They stifle their resentment.

Marsha and Tammy: One friend doing all the work and the other coasting illustrates the compliant/nonresponsive conflict. One party feels frustrated and resentful; the other wonders what the problem is. Marsha senses that the friendship isn't as important to Tammy as it is to her.

Boundaries and Your Spouse

Margo and Rob: One of the most important elements that promotes intimacy between two people is the ability of each to take responsibility for his or her own *feelings*.

Jim and Michelle: Both Jim and Michelle had needs. Problems arise when we make someone else responsible for our needs and *desires*, and when we blame them for our disappointments.

Bob and Nancy: Our spouse is not responsible for our *limits*; we are. Only we know what we can and want to give, and only we can be responsible for drawing that line. If we do not draw it, we can quickly become resentful.

Boundaries and Your Children

How we approach boundaries and childrearing will have an enormous impact on the character of our kids. If we teach responsibility, setting limits, and the delay of gratification early on, the smoother our children's later years of life will be.

Boundaries and Work

Favors and sacrifices are part of the Christian life; enabling is not. Learn to tell the difference by seeing if your giving is helping the other to become better or worse. The Bible requires responsible action out of the one who is given to. If you do not see responsible action after a season, set limits.

Solving Boundary Conflicts

You can solve boundary conflicts you encounter by taking specific steps:

1. *Identify the symptom.*

2. *Identify the origins or root causes of the symptom* (unmet needs, unrecognized fears, unresolved fears, etc.).

3. *Identify the boundary conflict.* Consider, for instance, which Law of Boundaries is being violated, who is taking responsibility for whom, or what consequences aren't being enforced.

4. *Identify who needs to take responsibility in the situation and the need that drives the conflict.*

5. *Take in the good.* God will often meet your needs through his people, but you must humble yourself, reach out to a good support system, and take in the good they offer you. You may be clumsy at first, but you can learn to respond to and receive love.

6. *Practice setting limits with safe people.* Begin saying no by practicing with people in your support group who will love and respect your boundaries.

7. *Say no to the bad.* Avoid hurtful situations and people who abused and controlled you in the past.

8. *Forgive.* Setting people who have hurt you free from an old debt is to stop wanting something from them; it sets you free as well.

Talking Together

Boundary Building

Dr. Townsend, Dr. Cloud, and people like those you have met in this curriculum have shown us how important it is to establish and maintain healthy boundaries with our family, our friends, our spouse, our children, and our coworkers. Now we're going to look more closely at each of these five areas of boundary conflicts.

Choose one of the following five areas of boundary conflicts we just learned about (pages 89–100) and take 15 minutes to read through and answer the questions for that particular category. If you don't have time to answer all the questions in the section, be sure to answer the last one. It asks you to write down one thing you have learned about yourself and one goal you have set for yourself. After 15 minutes, we'll take 10 more minutes for you to share with another person what each of you learned about yourself and the goal you set for yourself. You might even take a few of those 10 minutes to pray for each other.

Boundaries and Your Family

1. What choices have you made that your parents let you know, in one way or another, they don't fully approve of? Have you made these choices on the inside as well as the outside? Or do you feel guilty, apologetic, or uneasy about your choices? Explain.

2. Where do you need to loosen ties with your family of origin? What specific steps will you take to strengthen ties or forge new ones with the family that was created by your marriage?

3. Are you an adult financially? Support your answer with specific details about your life. What, if any, life-management functions are you allowing your parents to still perform for you?

4. *Triangulation* is a term that refers to the failure to resolve a conflict between two persons and the pulling in of a third to take sides. Is this a pattern in your family of origin that you've carried into your adult life? What conflict do you need to resolve directly right now?

5. Do you feel responsible for your parents? Is it unhealthy or is it a biblical, healthy responsibility (1 Tim. 5:3 – 4)? Are you still holding an allegiance to your earthly parents or have you fully become part of God's family and are now obeying his ways (Matt. 12:46 – 50; 23:9; Gal. 4:1 – 7)? Give specific evidence supporting your answer.

6. What is God saying to you personally through this lesson about boundaries, families of origin, and the family you've entered by marriage? And what will you do in response?

Lesson I learned about myself:

Boundary-building goal:

Boundaries and Your Friends

1. What role do you tend to take in a friendship—compliant, avoidant, manipulative, or nonresponsive? Why?

2. What does Romans 8:1 suggest about a strong basis for a friendship? When has being "in Christ Jesus" strengthened one of your friendships? When, for instance, has it helped you weather the storm of disappointment, hurt, or even betrayal? Be specific.

3. What keeps you connected to your friends? Their performance? Their lovability? Your guilt? Your sense of obligation? Something else? See 1 John 4:12.

4. In what relationship(s) have you been the minister, the rescuer, or the strong one without needs? Why do you think you chose that role for yourself? In what relationships(s) have you been able to ask for things for yourself (James 4:2)? What did you ask for and receive? If you don't yet feel comfortable asking for things you need, find a safe relationship where you can learn and practice this skill.

5. In what friendship have you become aware of or been confronted about your self-centeredness? Describe that moment of revelation or interaction and how you have benefited from that uncomfortable but important lesson about yourself.

6. What is God saying to you personally through this lesson about boundaries, ministries, and nurturing friendships? And what will you do in response?

Lesson I learned about myself:

Boundary-building goal:

Boundaries and Your Spouse

1. What feelings are you able to express in your marriage (2 Cor. 6:13)? What feelings would you like to be able to express? What do you tend to do rather than express your feelings to your spouse? How does that behavior affect your relationship with your spouse? What feelings do you need to take responsibility for today and share with your spouse?

2. Desires—like feelings—are another element of personhood for which each spouse needs to take responsibility (James 4:1–2). What conflicting wants do you and your spouse need to work out?

3. Often people will do more for their spouse than they really want to—and then resent him/her for allowing them to be a rescuer or to give for the wrong reasons. Where do you need to set some limits on what you will give your spouse? Where do you need to take responsibility for your own wants instead of expecting your spouse to take care of them for you?

4. Which of your actions, if any, is your spouse not letting you suffer the consequences for? What actions do you need to let your spouse suffer the consequences for? What is keeping you from letting your spouse suffer the consequences of his or her behavior?

5. Where are you waiting to be rescued rather than taking responsibility for yourself? Where are you giving in to your spouse's anger, pouting, and disappointments and thereby taking responsibility for what he or she is feeling? Where are you rescuing your spouse (see Prov. 19:19)? Explain the difference between being responsible *to* your spouse and responsible *for* him or her. Where do you need to show responsibility in your marriage today? What evil do you see and need to confront?

6. Where are you not respecting your spouse's boundaries, feelings, or choices? In what ways are you being controlling?

7. What is God saying to you personally through this lesson about boundaries, communication, and your spouse? And what will you do in response?

Lesson I learned about myself:

Boundary-building goal:

Boundaries and Your Children

1. What have your children learned about boundaries up to this point? How do your children respond when others set limits on them? Do they have a tantrum or sulk? Do they comply in order to keep the peace?

2. What are you doing to teach your children responsibility, limit-setting, and delay of gratification?

3. The positive facets of discipline are proactivity, prevention, and instruction (Eph. 6:4). Give specific examples of discipline that uses each of these positive aspects and make them appropriate to the ages and behaviors of your children.

   The negative facets of discipline are correction, chastisement, and consequences (Prov. 15:10). Give specific examples of discipline that uses each of these negative aspects and again make them appropriate to the ages and behaviors of your children.

Give an example of how you could use consequences to help set limits for your children. Use a specific situation you are currently dealing with.

4. What is your understanding of the difference between discipline (Heb. 12:10) and punishment (Rom. 6:23; James 2:10)? In what areas are your children currently practicing setting boundaries? How is your discipline helping them? Where could you be using consequences to give your children the chance to practice and learn?

5. What does it mean to you and your efforts to grow in building and maintaining boundaries that God will not judge you or withdraw his love from you? As they practice the various skills of life, do your children know that you will not judge them or withdraw your love from them? Support your answer.

6. What is God saying to you personally through this lesson about boundaries, your parenting, and your children? And what will you do in response?

Lesson I learned about myself:

Boundary-building goal:

Boundaries and Work

1. What work do you do? What does Paul command believers in Colossians 3:23? How could doing your work as "for the Lord" impact, if not revolutionize, your work?

2. What aspects of your work reflect God's activities? How is God using your work to make you more like Christ?

3. What problems in the workplace are you currently facing?

- Getting saddled with another person's responsibilities
- Working too much overtime
- Having misplaced priorities while on the job
- Difficult coworkers
- Critical attitudes
- Expecting too much of work
- Taking work-related stress home
- Disliking your job

4. Consider what you are learning about boundaries in this study. What lessons can you apply to the situation(s) you just identified?

5. God wants you to discover and use your gifts to his glory. He will also hold you accountable for what you do. What promise do you find in Psalm 37:4–5? What warning do you find in Ecclesiastes 11:9?

6. Where are you not respecting the boundaries of your coworkers? In what ways is your laziness, irresponsibility, or disobedience impacting others?

7. What is God saying to you personally through this lesson about boundaries, ministry, and work? And what will you do in response?

   Lesson I learned about myself:

   Boundary-building goal:

Exploring Together

The Importance of Establishing Boundaries

As promised, we've talked today about the importance of establishing boundaries with family members, friends, our spouse, our children, and our coworkers.

- We've seen that we need to make choices on the inside as well as the outside, especially when we're trying to separate from our family of origin.

- We've looked at what happens in friendships when people don't have or don't maintain healthy boundaries.

- We saw some marriages in trouble because the individuals didn't take responsibility for their feelings, desires, or limits.

- Gerald and Shannon's experience with Robby reminded us that boundaries are important for our kids, too. How we approach boundaries and childrearing will have an enormous impact on their character. We need to be teaching them responsibility, limit-setting, and delay of gratification.

- We also saw that boundaries are critical in the workplace. We need to do our job at the office, and helping others out is part of the Christian life, but enabling is not. We must discern if our giving is helping a coworker become better or worse.

Praying Together

One final word before we close in prayer. In the next session we'll start by sharing highlights of sessions 1–7. Each of you will have the opportunity to share something that has been especially meaningful or helpful to you. The questions on page 104 of this book may give you some ideas about what you might share. Let's pray.

> *God, you know that, for us sinners who are living in a fallen world, the potential for boundary conflict is great. Thank you for wanting to help us resolve conflict whenever it arises.*
>
> *Give each of us the courage and wisdom we need to take steps toward resolving boundary problems with our family members and friends. Help us clearly define our boundaries with our family members—and then help us do a good job maintaining those boundaries. And teach us to love our friends the way we want to be loved—with the unconditional and grace-filled love that you offer us.*
>
> *Help us learn to be more honest with ourselves and more honest about taking responsibility for our feelings, desires, attitudes, behaviors, choices, values, and limits with our*

spouse. Help us communicate our boundaries clearly and unapologetically. And help us take the risks we need to take in our marriage, knowing that you will be with us.

Teach us to live out all that we've heard about boundaries so that we can be helpful and effective role models for our children. Help us be wise about letting consequences be teachers, and give us the courage to let our children experience their failures.

Also guide us as we set boundaries in the workplace. Thank you for the work you've called us to do. May we honor you in our work.

Finally, God, thank you for helping us establish and live according to healthy boundaries. We pray in Jesus' name, Amen.

Suggested Reading

For more thoughts on this session's topic, read chapters 7 – 11 in the book *Boundaries*: "Boundaries and Your Family," "Boundaries and Your Friends," "Boundaries and Your Spouse," "Boundaries and Your Children," and "Boundaries and Work."

Boundary Successes, Part I

*I*n this session you will:

- Learn more about successfully establishing and maintaining healthy boundaries
- Look at six measurements you can take to determine your growth and development toward mature boundaries

Talking Together

A Quick Look Back

As I mentioned at the end of our last session, we'll begin today by reviewing the ground we've covered in our seven meetings together. Rather than discussing specific questions from each session or going back to read certain passages, you will have an opportunity to share what, in general, have been the highlights of our time together.

- What new understanding about boundaries, about relationships, or about family dynamics have you gained?
- What "aha!" experience have you had? When did a lightbulb go on?
- What has God shown you about yourself? about himself?
- What practical aspect of the teaching is already making a difference in your life?
- What has been revolutionary or life-changing about your study of boundaries so far?

Learning Together

DVD Segment: "Measuring Boundary Growth"

It's exciting to hear what God has been doing in your lives as a result of your study of boundaries. This week and next we will be learning more about successfully establishing and maintaining healthy boundaries. Today we'll look at six measurements you can take to determine your growth and development toward mature boundaries.

Specific, orderly changes herald the emergence of mature boundaries. In fact, you can measure the progression from Point A (boundarylessness) to Point B (mature boundaries). Right now we'll look at six indications of your growth in boundary development.

- *Measurement #1: Resentment, our early-warning signal.* One of the first signs that you are beginning to develop boundaries is a sense of resentment, frustration, or anger at the subtle and not-so-subtle violations in your life. Just as radar will signal the approach of a foreign missile, your anger can alert you to boundary violations in your life.

- *Measurement #2: A change of taste—becoming drawn to boundary-lovers.* As boundary-injured individuals begin developing their own boundaries, they become attracted to people who can hear their no without being critical and without getting hurt—people who will simply say, "Okay. See you next time."

  When we find relationships in which we have the freedom to set limits, something wonderful happens: in addition to the freedom to say no, we find the freedom to say a wholehearted, unconflicted, gratitude-driven yes to others.

- *Measure #3: Joining the family.* Joining the boundaried family is important mainly because, as with any spiritual discipline, boundaries can't be worked on in a vacuum. Furthermore, knowing we have a spiritual and emotional home somewhere helps us keep firm boundaries.

- *Measurement #4: Treasuring our treasures.* In order to further develop and strengthen healthy boundaries, we need to begin to value what we are responsible for—our feelings, talents, thoughts, attitudes, behavior, body, and the resources God has entrusted to us. This valuing—saying that these treasures matter and deciding to pay attention to them—helps us take the steps we need to take in order to protect those treasures and grow in them. After all, what you value in life is what you will invest in (Matt. 6:21).

- *Measurement #5: Practicing baby no's.* It is important to take baby steps toward communicating our new boundaries. A good place to start is with a support group or good friends. A good, supportive relationship cherishes the no of all parties involved. So start practicing your no with people who will honor it and love you for it.

- *Measurement #6: Rejoicing in the guilty feelings.* Often a sign that you are becoming a boundaried person is a sense of self-condemnation or critical self-judgment. The culprit here is an overactive, inaccurate, and unbiblically harsh internal judge. Because of this overactive judge, a boundary-injured individual has great difficulty setting limits. The activation of this hostile conscience, however, is a sign of spiritual growth because it means you are defying an incorrect authority (that hostile conscience) in order to obey God.

Talking Together

Measuring Boundary Growth

Now let's look more closely at each of these six signs of growth as they pertain to our ability to set and maintain boundaries.

Measurement #1: Resentment, our early-warning signal

1. Why is resentment, frustration, or anger a signal that someone has violated one of your boundaries? See Proverbs 29:11.

2. How can anger—unrecognized and unexpressed—affect our day-to-day lives?

Boundary Building ... On Your Own

For You to Do After This Session and Before the Next One

What experiences or relationships have helped you—or are helping you—get in touch with your anger, resentment, or frustration and enabled you to see that you want to be treated differently?

Measurement #2: A change of tastes — becoming drawn to boundary-lovers

1. Define "boundary-buster." Discuss how someone who has difficulty setting boundaries in his or her own life can be drawn to boundary-busters and see them as "normal."

2. What freedoms come in relationships with boundary-lovers?

Boundary Building ... On Your Own

For You to Do After This Session and Before the Next One

1. In the past, how have you responded to people who can say a clear no? How do you respond now? How do you want to respond?

2. Who are the boundary-lovers in your life? If your list is short, where will you go to find some boundary-lovers?

Measurement #3: Joining the family

1. Explain why it is critical to join the "boundaried family" and have supportive relationships as you develop and strengthen your boundaries. Consider Jesus' words in Matthew 18:20.

2. Where can you go to find supportive, safe relationships?

Boundary Building ... On Your Own

For You to Do After This Session and Before the Next One

1. When has the friendship of someone with similar values helped you stand strong? Be specific.

2. Why could (or does) being part of a boundaried family help you with your boundaries?

Measurement #4: Treasuring our treasures

1. What are some of the consequences of taking responsibility for anyone other than yourself?

2. Why is it important to value ourselves and treasure our treasures? Answer this question in terms of stewardship and responsibility.

Boundary Building ... On Your Own

For You to Do After This Session and Before the Next One

1. Scripture teaches that "we love because [God] first loved us" (1 John 4:19). In other words, we learn to be loving because we are loved. As a child, what did you learn about your worth, your lovableness? As a result of those childhood lessons, how well do you take care of yourself — your feelings, talents, thoughts, attitudes, behavior, body, and the resources God has entrusted to you? Support this answer with details from your life.

2. Begin a list of your "treasures" — your time, money, feelings, and beliefs. How do you want others to treat them? How do you want others to *not* treat them?

Measurement #5: Practicing baby no's

1. What are some effective ways of saying no or telling the truth? Come up with responses for the following situations:

   - A church acquaintance asks you to serve on yet another committee

   - A good friend needs to talk right now, just as you've started the promised reading time with your young child

   - Your neighbor asks for your honest opinion about a new (and disastrous) haircut

   - Your irresponsible coworker asks you to take on some additional work which will enable him or her to complete a report assigned long ago and due tomorrow

   - Your accountant suggests that you fudge on your taxes or a coworker encourages you to be less than honest on your expense report

2. In what current real-life situation do you need to say no or be a truth-teller? Choose the words — and practice saying them now.

Boundary Building ... On Your Own

For You to Do After This Session and Before the Next One

1. What past injuries make setting limits and saying no difficult for you?

2. With whom can you practice saying no (Lev. 19:17; Prov. 10:18)?

3. What support group and/or good friend(s) will you ask if you could work on boundaries with them? When will you make that request?

Measurement #6: Rejoicing in the guilty feelings

1. Why do people who are starting to set boundaries often feel guilt and self-condemnation—and why is that feeling a good sign?

2. What is the source of an overactive but inaccurate conscience, with its guilt-inducing "how could you?" messages? What steps can a person take to silence that enslaving voice?

Boundary Building ... On Your Own

For You to Do After This Session and Before the Next One

1. What evidence is there that you have an overactive and harsh internal judge? Give specific examples of the condemning self-talk that goes on in your mind—or refer to people who have helped you recognize that critical internal voice for what it is.

2. In what boundary setting will you feel like you are transgressing when you aren't? What are you going to do with that guilt?

Exploring Together

Reviewing Boundary Measurements

Let's review what we have learned today about measurements for boundaries.

- Resentment is our early-warning signal, making us aware that someone is violating our boundaries.

- A change of taste indicates that we are attracted to, rather than put off by, boundary-lovers.

- Joining the boundaried family provides us a safe place to practice our no's and maintain our boundaries.

- When we begin treasuring our treasures, we can see that we are letting ourselves receive the love we need in order to begin loving ourselves and others in a freer, more biblical way.

- We start practicing baby no's when we feel supported and therefore ready to communicate our new boundaries.

- As we communicate those limits and say those no's, we feel guilty — and we rejoice in those feelings, celebrating the growth and the freedom from unbiblical restraints that the guilt indicates.

Praying Together

Now let's close our time together with prayer.

Lord, you know where each of us is on this journey toward healthy boundaries. You know the steps we've taken, and you know what lies ahead.

Thank you for creating in us the anger that helps us identify boundary violations. Teach us to pay attention to those internal signals.

Open our eyes to the boundary-lovers around us and help us learn from them. Thank you for the support group of boundary-lovers that you have prepared for each of us and for the valuable lessons and love the people in that family offer us.

Thank you, too, for loving us and for the fact that, despite any childhood lessons about our lack of worth we may have learned, we can find worth in you. Help us value our treasures. Give us courage to practice our baby no's—and wisdom as we choose people to practice with.

Thank you for showing us the meaning of the guilt we feel when we start building boundaries. We know that your rules for living are better than the guilt-generating rules we learned growing up.

Please keep us learning about boundaries and growing in our ability to establish and maintain them. We pray in Jesus' name, Amen.

Suggested Reading

For more thoughts on this session's topic, read the first half of chapter 15 (through Step #6) in the book *Boundaries*: "How to Measure Success with Boundaries."

Session 9

Boundary Successes, Part II

*I*n this session you will:

- Look briefly at the five remaining measurable indications of growth toward healthy boundaries
- Reflect on where you are in your development of boundaries

117

Learning Together

DVD Segment #1: "Success with Boundaries"

Last week we looked at six specific changes that herald the emergence of mature boundaries. Today we'll begin by looking briefly at five other measurable indicators of growth toward healthy boundaries. These measurements (eleven in all) can help you see where you are in your development of boundaries and guide you to the next step.

- *Measurement #7: Practicing grown-up no's.* There comes a time when you need to deal with the extremely complicated and even frightening relationships and situations in your life and practice grown-up no's. You need to deal with your number-one "boundary buster" and the people in your life with whom it's difficult for you to set limits. Straightening out these relationships is a major goal in becoming a boundaried person. Setting important limits with such significant people and in significant circumstances involving key life issues is the fruit of much work and maturity. And our real target is maturity: the ability to love successfully and work successfully, the goal of having a character structure that has boundaries and that can set limits on self and others at the appropriate times, the goal of becoming more like Christ.

- *Measurement #8: Rejoicing in the absence of guilty feelings.* With consistent work and good support, we will find that the guilt we feel when we set boundaries eventually diminishes. That point comes when we have shifted from listening to our overactive conscience and respond instead according to the biblical values of love, responsibility, and forgiveness. These values will have been reinforced by many, many experiences with loving, truthful people who understand boundaries.

- *Measurement #9: Loving the boundaries of others.* If we expect others to respect our boundaries, we need to respect theirs. First, when we are concerned about protecting the treasures of others, we work against the self-centeredness that is part of our fallen nature. Second, loving others' boundaries increases our capacity to care about others. It isn't difficult to love the agreeable parts of people. It's another story, however, when we encounter resistance, confrontation, or separateness. Loving others stretches those muscles.

- *Measurement #10: Freeing our no and our yes.* Learn not to promise too much before you have done your spiritual and emotional calculations. When you're not sure about something, say no. It is more responsible to give out of our resources than to promise that which we might not be able to deliver. And freeing your no like that also frees your yes. When you can say no without conflict, you can freely—without resentment and without being motivated by guilt—say yes to love and service.

- *Measurement #11: Value-driven goal setting.* The ultimate goal of learning boundaries is to free us up to protect, nurture, and develop the life God has given us. Individuals with mature boundaries have a direction in life. They make choices based not on the fear of other people's reactions, but on what they believe to be important for their life. Their goals are not based on emotion but values. They plan ahead, understanding and allowing for resistance to boundaries and goals and ultimately experiencing the joy of desires fulfilled. People with mature limits know that, should it be needed, a no is waiting inside the heart to be used to protect and develop their time, talents, and treasures.

Talking Together

Success with Boundaries

As we did last week, we're going to spend some time talking about these signs of boundary development. Let's look more closely at each of these five measurements of growth.

Measurement #7: Practicing grown-up no's

1. According to 1 John 3:2 ("Dear friends, now we are children of God, and what we will be has not yet been made known. But we know that when he appears, we shall be like him, for we shall see him as he is"), what is the ultimate goal of boundary work? Why are grown-up no's essential to reaching that goal?

2. Why should a person practicing grown-up no's have some support?

Boundary Building ... On Your Own

For You to Do in the Coming Days

1. Who is your number-one "boundary buster"? Who else makes the list of boundary busters in your life?

2. What specific treasures are being violated in your relationships with these people?

3. What specific boundaries do you need to set to protect those treasures?

Measurement #8: Rejoicing in the absence of guilty feelings

1. What kinds of experiences can help quiet the voice of a harsh internal parent?

2. Are you noticing an easing up of guilty feelings and an increase of empathetic sorrow? Point to a specific instance of setting limits that might have caused you greater guilt and more self-recriminations had it happened awhile back.

Boundary Building ... On Your Own

For You to Do in the Coming Days

Identify some of the people God has placed in your life as well as some of the experiences that have helped quiet your harsh internal parent.

Measurement #9: Loving the boundaries of others

1. We are commanded to love our neighbors as ourselves (Gal. 5:14). What does this command mean when it comes to other people's boundaries?

2. Before people start setting boundaries, how do they tend to respond to the boundaries of others? Why?

Boundary Building ... On Your Own

For You to Do in the Coming Days

1. How do you tend to respond to other people's boundaries?

2. How would you like to respond to their boundaries?

Measurement #10: Freeing our no and our yes

1. Why does freeing our no also free our yes?

2. What often happens when people say yes out of guilt or compliance? How do they feel if they live out their yes?

Boundary Building ... On Your Own

For You to Do in the Coming Days

What do you plan to do the next time someone asks you for something you aren't sure you can give?

Measurement #11: Value-driven goal setting

1. What impact do boundaries—or a lack of them—have on the pace of life?

2. Explain why healthy boundaries are a matter of good stewardship of the life with which God has gifted us. Why do mature and wise boundaries bear the joyful fruit of desires fulfilled?

Boundary Building ... On Your Own

For You to Do in the Coming Days

1. Does your life tend toward a frantic or a steady pace? Does life feel in a hurry or out of control? Or do you feel as if you're making steady progress toward a goal? How do your boundaries—or lack of them—contribute to the state of your life?

2. What are you doing to stand strong against resistance to boundaries? What weapons do you now have in your arsenal?

Learning Together

DVD Segment #2: "Sherrie with Boundaries"

Do you remember meeting Sherrie in our first session? Let's see what she's learned about setting healthy boundaries.

- In session 1, Sherrie stumbled through the day in a haphazard, out-of-control fashion. But Sherrie has restructured her life, adding boundaries, setting limits, and living within those.

- Sherrie's day is now characterized by the freedom, self-control, and intimacy that result from a lifestyle based on a healthy understanding of boundaries.

- Sherrie's example is not a fairy-tale fantasy. It's a real-life experience that you yourself can experience or perhaps already are experiencing. Like Sherrie, you can learn to take ownership of your life. You can learn what things are your responsibility and what aren't. You can stop taking on problems that God never intended you to take on. You can learn to live by healthy boundaries and experience the relationships and achieve the purposes that God intends for you.

Exploring Together

The Benefits of Healthy Boundaries

Like Sherrie, you yourself can experience—and perhaps already are experiencing—the kinds of positive changes that come with healthy boundaries. Let's look at some of the benefits of healthy boundaries:

- Healthier sleep patterns
- Better relationships with family members
- A diet and exercise program that works for you
- The perspective that dieting and exercise is good stewardship, not selfishness
- More effective parenting skills: bedtimes for the children; shared household tasks; letting them be responsible for getting to the carpool ride on time
- Well-guarded family time
- A more fulfilling and joy-filled marriage: parenting together; setting limits with your spouse and standing by clearly defined consequences; being more of a team with a new sense of mutual love and mutual responsibility; being unafraid of conflict, forgiving of each other's mistakes, and respectful of each other's boundaries
- Clear limits on and wiser choices of church commitments
- A stronger relationship with God
- A solid support group

Maybe you're already seeing progress in some of these areas. Be sure to thank God, as Sherrie did, for that blessing.

Talking Together

A Wrap-Up

Setting and maintaining clear boundaries in life requires hard work and risk-taking, but you'll definitely find the effort worth it. Let's talk for a few minutes about how far we've come in our own boundary building and where we'd like to continue to grow.

1. Consider the benefits of healthy boundaries listed on page 126. Where have you seen progress in your own life?

2. In which of the areas listed do you still have work to do? What boundary work are you doing in those areas? Be specific about your plan and your current efforts in regard to those issues.

Praying Together

Like Sherrie, you can learn to take ownership of your life. You can learn what things are your responsibility and what aren't. You can stop taking on problems God never intended you to take on. You can learn to live by healthy boundaries and experience the relationships and achieve the purposes that God intends for you. May God bless you as you continue on the journey we've been traveling together for nine weeks. Let's pray.

God, we praise you that you are with us always and that you work in our hearts and lives to heal and to free us, to teach and to mold us. Give us courage to confront the boundary busters in our life with grown-up no's. Teach us to love others as ourselves and to respect their boundaries the way we want them to respect ours. And teach us to count the cost when we see an opportunity to give — and then to freely say yes or just as freely say no.

Help each of us learn to take ownership of our life. Teach us to see what is our responsibility and what isn't. Show us what problems we've taken on that you never intended us to. And guide us as we try to establish and live by biblical boundaries.

As we go from this study, heavenly Father, continue the good work you have begun in us. May we persevere in this challenging path of growth, trusting in the truth of your Word, the presence of your Spirit, and the love of your people. We pray in Jesus' name, Amen.

Suggested Reading

For more thoughts on this session's topic, read the second half of chapter 15 (from Step #7 onward) in the book *Boundaries*: "How to Measure Success with Boundaries."